The Way of the Unicorn
An introduction to Unicorn Light Mysticism

AHURA Z. DILIIZA

To Anita and Jorge
Family is always
and you are definately
family. Love
Ahura Z

DEDICATION

I dedicate this book to my teachers and my family (my family being those that choose to evolve and grow with me and grow and expand with Universal positivity).

May the Unicorn's horn light your way and shield you against all things evil. *Namaste.*

CONTENTS

INTRODUCTION TO UNICORN LIGHT MYSTICISM

The Unicorn has forever been a symbol of magic and beauty. In our childhood it was the Unicorn that made us believe that it was possible to live a life of wonder, mysticism and peace. When I was a child I dreamt of walking in fields of green grass and smelling trees that were heavy with fruit. There was always a rainbow, a waterfall and a Golden Unicorn. This place in my dreams was the only place that I felt safe. I knew then that anything was possible, even to catch a rainbow. It is this that moved me to learn the ways of magic, and create Unicorn Light Mysticism.

The Unicorn has been a constant symbol of my life and, like it, I have striven to be the embodiment of hope. Wherever it walks there is peace and safety. By its very nature it cancels out evil. This is what I wanted to do. To bring peace, magic and safety to all. One day as I looked at my reflection in the mirror I saw the Unicorn – only this time it was also me – and like a lightning bolt it hit me; I made the realization that the Unicorn and myself were one, and that I could be the very thing that I most loved. I thought that I was following a Unicorn, but in truth the Unicorn was me.

In this introduction you will learn very valuable incantations and spells. However, The Way of The Unicorn is not all spells and incantations. It is also thinking and perception. If you are looking to change something in your life you must understand that to a degree your life will change globally.

You see, in order to even approach the throne of Unicorn Light Mysticism we must learn practicality. We must learn basic mysticism which is called "common sense." Even in my early formal training one of the first magical disciplines that I was to learn was to keep a job for a year. Seems pretty easy right? Remember that I am a telepath, and as a young man I was prone to those things that any young man was. Although I knew things, staying grounded and keeping my feet on the ground (let alone controlling the constant informational input from all around me) often proved troublesome (especially when someone is speaking to you but your inner ear hears something entirely different). I couldn't keep a job because I couldn't keep my big telepathic mouth shut. My teacher's first directive to me was to get a job, hold it and to keep my mouth shut. "Do what is expected of you to do, and then leave."

Because of following that directive I could eat, pay bills, afford basic things such as clothes, rent, outings, without having to borrow money from friends, which meant that I could concentrate on other things. So the best magic that I learned was common sense.

As a practitioner of Unicorn Light Mysticism we must respect the beliefs of all walks of life, so long as they are positive. The Universe is an ever expanding opportunity to experience and learn, and we as evolving human beings owe it to ourselves to take part in that expansion therefore to be acquainted with all philosophies and/or religions is as much a part of education as is psychic development and spell work. Your education also includes what we in the metaphysical community call the "Divine Sciences" Some of these sciences include: astrology, numerology, psychometry, palmistry, and vibrational frequency.   Also psychic self-defense.

- Astrology – the logistics of the stars and planets and their effects on our everyday existence.
- Numerology – the study of numbers.
- Palmistry – the study of the lines and shape of the hands, and what they reveal.
- Psychometry – the ability to touch an object and feel the actual energy of it.
- Vibrational frequency – to detect, regulate and change the vibratory energy of a person place or thing.
- Psychic self defense – he art of protecting ones life, and life energy against black magic and psychic attack.

The very premise of Unicorn Light Mysticism is to cancel or banish evil magic and spells and to enhance the lives of the practitioner. The magic that I will give you is meant to create and promote good and light. Although as we have pointed out earlier energy is energy until it is formed and directed, the directive and alignment of Unicorn Light Mysticism is "good" and therefore effective ONLY in accordance with that principal.

The spells, incantations and thoughts that are contained in this book are designed to lead the reader to their own realization. It is my hope that each will find within them that which is the birthright of all woman- and man-kind: the discovery that we have written within us the way of magic, the way of the metaphysical... *The Way of The Unicorn.*

Class is in session.

AHURA Z. DILIIZA

1 THE BODIES

Let us begin with the bodies, as it is with these we humans have a remarkable fascination. The body that you were given to live in is merely a tool. Much like a car or truck, it gets you from point *a* to point *b*.

Most of us have been taught that this is the only body that we have, and that there is nothing that we can do about it. But I say thee, nay! There are four more to go along with that one. You actually have five "bodies" that live simultaneously and function perfectly on both a conscious and unconscious level. Each exists on a different plane (or dimension, as you will) but they are all you. These bodies are:

The Physical Body

The physical body; a perfect bio-mechanical unit comprised of carbon, oxygen, hydrogen, and a combination of minerals that are hyper charged by a group of elements (which we will cover later) to cause a combination of reactions, responses, and dynamics which enable you to move, breathe, and function on a normal day to day basis.

In essence, even your physical body is a living example of alchemical and mystical manipulation, manifestation, and animation. In other words, "magic".

Even if we were to compare the physical body to the symbology of magic we would find a strange coincidence. Leonardo Da Vinci depicted a man in a five pointed stance which, even scientifically, matches the pentacle, or five pointed Star. Each extremity representing a body, element, sense, and dimension culminating into one being.

The Astral Body

The second body that you have is called the *astral* body. This body actually fits over your physical body much like a glove, encasing and even protecting your physical body. It is this body that you can learn a great deal from, but at the same time learn to protect, as it has a tendency to leave sometimes – unconsciously – the physical body, in the event of trauma or stress.

The astral body exists on a corresponding dimension, or astral realm that, although lacking physical tangibility, is every bit as real as the physical dimension. There is color, shape, depth, and even texture to this realm. It is where one is more than likely to have an encounter with beings that are without a physical body, or even beings from other kingdoms, (elementals, changelings, etc.).

Many have tried with some success to harness the ability to enter into this realm for short periods of time in order to find answers or seek guidance from one or more of the vast amounts of residents that live there, for the purpose of spiritual or personal development. Unfortunately, what the average novice or practitioner does not know, or even thinks about, is the nature of the astral realm. It is seductive, unstable, chaotic and, like nitroglycerin can explode in one's face.

For those that wish to delve onto the astral ocean, it is advisable to take into consideration these points:

1. There are many beings that live there that have no body, and know that they need a body in order to complete their Evolutionary process.
2. Because of the lack of physical limitation, these same beings can assume any shape that they please, even if only temporarily.
3. Because of the lack of mental barriers in the astral realm, your thoughts are like beacons of light to these inhabitants, as are your fantasies, so it might be dangerous to assume that you are speaking with whom you think you are speaking.
4. The seductive nature of the astral realm can lead one into an almost obsessive state, causing one to want to be overly comfortable with the astral, and unbalanced in the physical, resulting in a sort of neurosis, much like the heroin or opium addict. Not to mention the fixation on certain beings that emulate or copy someone that the practitioner has taken a fancy to in the physical realm, causing them to believe that there is a relationship between the practitioner and the physical being (which has been the case in many stalking cases). The practitioner loses his/her grip on the tangible, is at the mercy of fantasy, and can be ultimately lost to their own desire

5. In order to visit the astral realm one has to use massive amounts of energy to stay. Although it appears that one is merely resting, the astral body is draining itself, and will begin to drain energy from the physical body (burning the furniture in order to keep the train running). This causes a parasitic dynamic between the astral body, and the physical body, and if the practitioner fails to "get a grip", then the physical body becomes weaker, and weaker. Signs of physical degeneration may be barely noticeable to the observer at first, but then as time marches on drastic physical changes will make themselves apparent. For those practitioners that do tangle with the astral web, here are some signs that the water has become too deep for you::
   a) Rapid loss of muscle mass and drop in body heat
   b) Rapid weight gain and lethargy accompanied by depression
   c) Abandoment of physical awareness and deceitfulness, accompanied by severe mood swings and the complete loss of common sense.

If this sounds familiar stay out of the astral realm!

These points being considered, the benefit of this realm are great. You can detect malady or sickness long before it registers on your physical body, which can afford you time to counteract the malady "astrally" and avoiding it altogether. First you are going to have to use something that is of the astral realm, while staying conscious. For lack of a better term, let us call this the *imagination*.

One has to understand this gift in order to use it, as it could very well be said that the astral body is the very fuel of the dream machine. That being said, we will move on until such a time that we can address the "how to" aspect of using the astral realm safely.

The Ethereal Body

The ethereal body is that which joins us all in a network of light, much like a spider's web, and has been called by "airy fairy-ists" the aura, the "white light", or the "halo". In truth it is merely the vibrational frequency field that each individual has that distinguishes one being from another. A signature, if you will, that emanates out from the body as rays of light emanate from the sun. Each person has a different color and pattern. Each has a sound and solidity, based upon the personality of the individual.

As was stated earlier we are still connected by what would appear (to those who could see it) white bands of light that seem to go from one person to anther and then connect to the very earth, moving endlessly between mother and child, husband and wife, friend and foe alike. We as human beings thrive on the ethereal field of the Earth, because she is not only our home, but also our source of food, shelter and make-up. Without the earth we would not exist, as the material that we are created from comes from "her" and goes back once we leave our physical form. Literally we are one with the Earth and with one another. When Jesus said *when a man commits and act in his heart it is as sure as committing it physically* he of course was speaking the truth, as we are ethereally joined.

The Spirit Body

The spirit body is, along with the soul, the most mystifying aspect and body. The spirit is the living principal force of life, and is indomitable. Contrary to a popular belief the spirit cannot be harmed by anyone or anything. It is that part of you that is totally and completely beyond vulnerability. So to say that something hurt your spirit, or your spirit is suffering is absolutely incorrect. You must understand that nothing, *absolutely nothing*, can harm your spirit. Not even YOU.

The Soul Body

The soul body is that which completes us as living beings. It is the force behind and in front of everything that we are, have been, and will ever be. It is the highest vibration of all bodies, and totally unfathomable (as is the spirit). It is the part of us that is music, art, love, dance, feeling and knowing, and that which gives breath to us all. This body, along with our spirit body, cannot be touched by you or anyone else, as the Universe in their grand wisdom knew that if we could touch our souls we'd only try to find a way to dominate it in ourselves and others (Universal fail-safe, you might call it). Thus our task is clear; if we as growing beings want to become more in tuned so as to be able to see our spirit or soul bodies, then we will evolve.

So until the time that we can perceive clearly these bodies, let it suffice to say your spirit and soul bodies are doing what they are supposed to do, and are the highest part of yourselves, hoping beyond hope that you will be interested enough to find out exactly what you're made of.

In essence we are much more that we have been led to think that we are, and are the very children of a force that has been around longer than even the most ancient among us could remember. The cloth and thread that the God/dess created all things from is Magic...

AHURA Z. DILIIZA

2 THE MINDS

Now that you have been introduced to the bodies it is time to be introduced to your minds. The five bodies correspond to five minds, and function uniquely and simultaneously. It has been said that we as human beings only use fifteen percent of our brains, but this also is a scientific *faux pas*. A theory has been introduced and quoted, in regards to something as simple as a candy bar, that the whole is greater than the sum total of its parts. But you need the parts in order for the whole to *be*, therefore, we can conclude that the brain is being used in its entirety in order for it to function correctly at all. Likewise you need five minds to run five bodies. These minds are...

The Conscious Mind

The conscious mind is the slowest of all your minds. It is the one that runs your physical body. Unfortunately, science has done little justice to this remarkable tool, as it is a mistake to think that the brain and the conscious mind are not the same. Understanding that the first body is physical, it should be elementary that a physical mind would be needed to run it. As the world we live in is physical, all things within it have a physical representation. The conscious mind, or brain, is designed to receive, process, repeat, and remember information. This particular mind, other than to run the physical, instinctual and automatic functions of the body, for all intent and purpose has no other function. It is merely the puppet-master to the bio-mechanical suit that houses your spirit and soul.

The Subconscious Mind

The sub conscious mind is perhaps the most misunderstood mind of all, as it has been mistaken for eons with another mind (that we will discuss later). The subconscious, or thinking mind, contrary to popular belief, is the mind that is responsible for perception, understanding, comprehension and concentration. Long has it been said that the subconscious mind can only discern colors, symbols, sounds and feelings. This is incorrect. The subconscious mind should actually be referred to as the upper learning center of the brain. In other words, the subconscious mind interprets what is unseen and unspoken, to that which can only comprehend what is seen and spoken (the conscious mind).

The Sub-subconscious Mind

The sub-subconscious mind is never really mentioned in science, or even psychological journals, as little to nothing is known about it in conventional medicine. This magnificent tool is the one that is responsible for "super human" acts, or seemingly miraculous mental feats of psychic phenomenon. It could literally be referred to as the psychic mind.

Now, technically speaking, since the whole of our planet operates within an electrically charged current that pervades everyone and everything, we as human beings would need the ability to, not only transform this electrical current, but to assimilate and use this current as a power source to run our bio-mechanical machine (physical body). Furthermore, we would need, again, a translator to interpret that which has only color, sound, vibration and formless energy to the upper learning center of the bio-mech at controlled intervals, so to avoid a massive overload and breakdown of both upper and lower biomechanical function. It is this that the sub-subconscious is responsible for. It is also this mind that has been mistaken by doctor and psychotherapist alike for the subconscious mind.

Metaphysically speaking the sub-subconscious, being in tune with the vibrational frequency of the earth, can deliver timely messages to us at any given moment. What we think is psychic phenomenon is merely the attempt of the sub-subconscious to "upgrade our system" in order to help us receive more of the information that is due to us as evolving beings. A bonus is when we are mentally available, the sub-subconscious can not only deliver messages of the future or past, but hyper-charge the bio-mechanical suit, enabling it to perform great feats of physical strength, speed and agility. For instance, a person is about to step off of a curb onto the street and instantly leaps back with speed not usually at their disposal, avoiding a speeding car. Or a mother that, upon seeing her child in danger, obtains the physical strength of ten, and as soon as the crisis is over returns to her normal state, yet not knowing how she could possibly have lifted a truck by herself. That is one prime example of how the sub-subconscious mind works.

It would seem that this mind is the interpreter of the cosmos, reminding us that we are more than we seem. All in all, you could say that this mind is the bridge between God and man.

The Sub-supraconscious Mind

It has been said that there are those that have waited their whole lives for just one moment of revelation, and upon receiving this have been changed for ever…

Thus is the semi-divine nature of the sub-supraconscious mind. This mind can be effectively named our own personal harbinger of change, for each time that it filters its powerful messages to us there is ineffably a complete change, not only in our mentality, but in our physicality as well. These rays of cosmic energy may last for only seconds but the effect can last for years depending upon ones reaction and response to them. It is this mind that makes us aware that there is more to life than what we are, and calls us to reach through the clouds of normality in response to something seemingly holy, and like the mythological siren beckons us to find it if we can.

Each time this mind flashes something is created; a song, a book, a painting, or even a new life. It is the prophecy of ourselves in the future, now complete with the energy to become that which we have seen. Would that we could only tap consciously into this resource there would be no war, famine, hate or sickness, for all one would have to do is to see, and be. Fortunately, we are given this very chance from time to time by the very mechanism that is the sub-supraconscious, and that in and of itself is a revelation.

The Supraconscious Mind

The supraconscious mind is the totality of all of your minds. It is the whole that is a living part of the great mind. It is that which has been called God- or Goddess-consciousness, and rightly so. It is where every inspiration, every motivation and inclination that has been shot like cosmic arrows from the divine bow of the universe is from. It is constant, untiring, and ever vigilant in its effort to help us to guide us to ourselves, in hope that we would be interested in knowing who we are, why we are, and what we are doing. This mind is the very wellspring that all knowledge comes from and will return to; it is your highest mind. That being said, it is important to understand that the supraconscious mind is not separate from you, but, like all of the other minds *is* you, and works simultaneously, directly and indirectly to bring you to your optimal state of being. It is the mental heaven to our mental earth, yet one does not exist without the other. The supraconscious mind is, for lack of a better word, Holy.

All five of the minds that have been introduced work dependently and simultaneously. There is no real way to separate them, as you will find the presence of one in all, and all in one. Suffice it to say that before one studies magic, one should know that the ability even to *think* is magic.

AHURA Z. DILIIZA

3 THE SENSES

Now that we have been introduced to the minds and bodies, it is time to be re-introduced to the senses. As we all know most people have five: hearing, seeing. smelling, tasting, and touching. These are merely sensory abilities, nervous impulses dictated by electro-magnetic flashes that translate a signal to and from our brains. In other words, these senses are standard equipment that comes with the vehicle we call the human body. In truth they are nothing more.

Touch

Often in our driven pursuit of power are we deceived, not only by our ambitions, but the very thing that we invest so much energy and time into. For instance, one might be offended by the words or actions of another based upon what was observed with one or more of our sensory input devices, "the senses". That same person will then approach the latter and say that person hurt his/her feelings. This is incorrect. The only sensory device that might qualify to "hurt" the feelings of another would be, if it were possible, the sense of touch. However "touching" and "feeling" are two different actions. To touch is merely to make contact with another physical entity or object, and the resulting physical sensation therein. There must always be a physical contact involved in touching. Always.

Now that we have identified touching let us identify the next culprit in our devised deception. To say that someone "hurt your feelings" is again incorrect because that which we have incorrectly called hurt "feelings" is based upon the non-physical contact, action or words of another individual. This particular deception is often mistaken for feelings. It is called the "emotion". Emotion is an instinctual combination of observation and sensation that is always, always, ALWAYS based on that which happens outside of ourselves (what someone did, what they didn't do, what they said or did not say) and always involves another.

Feelings on the other hand, have nothing to do with what another did or did not do to, with, against, or for you, as they are an expression of the soul and spirit borne of a compelling that may or may not happen at any given moment, and does not need physical stimulus in order to happen.

Smell

Now, all that being said, let us move on to another of the senses that is probably the most important, yet the most taken for granted of all: the olfactory sense, or sense of smell. This particular sense is actually the most influential of all. It and it alone can pervade the world of your vision, taste, hearing, and touch, and in many cases is the deciding factor when it comes to whether you like something or not. This sense has been known to invoke emotion and even memories both short and long term.

An example of how the olfactory sense works would be to pick a scent that is reminiscent of your mother or other loved-one. Curiously you will not only smell the scent, but you will see the image of the person who wore the scent, and in some cases hear them speaking to you.

For those that are students of the metaphysical this is a required experiment, as the olfactory sense, because of its magnificent pervasiveness, can be the key agent in breaking detrimental habits such as smoking, drinking and drug use, hence the amazingly resplendent interest in the art known to many as "aromatherapy" (which is probably more accurately termed "aroma-theism", but who are we to quibble?).

All in all, the olfactory sense gets the thumbs up in the most powerful sense group, and as we can deduce from its described properties, often instrumental in in psychic development.

Cultivated, this sense would be used in what is called "smell-seeing", often associated with psychic police work (the art of "sniffing out" negative vibrations and expelling them).

Taste

Our next stop will be in the zone of the sense of taste. This particular sense has its hooks in our ability to discriminate and discern.

How, you ask?

Well if we take into consideration the fact that we are creatures of habit, we will see that our habitual patterns are first based on instinct, beginning with our instinct to eat, and that instinct is colored with the assistance of the aforementioned olfactory sense, what tastes "good", or "bad" to us.

Even as children we decide that if it tastes good to us we will eat it and if it doesn't there is *no way* that we will eat it, even at the risk of not getting--yes that's right--desert, which almost always tastes good (except in those cases that your grandmother thinks it's a good idea to put a huge dollop of mayonnaise on jello! Yuck!). But even then it comes down to that wonderful sense...Taste.

As we grow into adulthood and (hopefully) mature, we develop these areas of "good" and "bad" to include what we call right and wrong, and base the majority of our judgment on these factors. We connect that which is "good" to what is right and likewise what is "bad" to wrong, and in many cases are right on point. That is, if the society you live in has also decided that what *you* think is right and wrong is good and bad as well. However, if not, then you are more than likely going to be put into a position where you have to either a.) try to convince someone that if they want desert then they will have to eat their peas, or b.) be convinced that jello with mayonnaise is a "good" thing. Either way you are STILL the child sitting in the instinctual chair of "taste".

Now, the physical sense of taste is located in the tongue (or so we are led to believe). And I will, for the sake of good ink and paper, forgo the tedious, outdated third-grade explanation of how the little taste buds do their job (even though without the olfactory sense they could not do justice), and let it suffice to say that the sense of taste enables us has human beings to define, not only our character, but our identification, and it is therefore powerful and essential to life as we know it.

Hearing

The sense of hearing is pretty self explanatory. We hear everything, in one way or another, based upon vibrational frequency and rate, combined with surface contact.

These vibrational frequencies, which are the actual movement of energy and the shape or speed thereof, are what constitutes tone. It is our ability to register this vibrational interaction that we call "hearing". What this means is that hearing doesn't only have to do with the ears, but with the entire body, even the skin.

Those who have ever had trouble hearing in their lives, as I have, can agree that if in fact the ears are malfunctioning, something else occurs to enable you to "register" the surrounding vibrations. It is as if the very air around you concentrates to form an "ethereal ear" in order for you to know what's happening.

The person that is labeled "deaf" is indeed mislabeled, for they are not deaf but merely hear things in a different way than what we as a society have deemed normal, and in many cases hear better than any of us with "normal" hearing.

Our ability to hear is, in truth and fact, the sense that we use in order to understand and comprehend. And in many ways, alongside with the sense of sight (which we will address next), helps us to identify who, what and where and is key in our ability to communicate.

Sight

On our magnificent journey through the world of the senses we make our last stop at the all-powerful sense of sight.

Isn't it amazing that I would use that particular phrase to introduce sight. *"ALL POWERFUL ful, ful, ful..."*.

You might think that I'm just joking, but indeed I am not, as whole societies have been born, destroyed, defined, deified, enslaved, chosen (not chosen), liked, disliked, strengthened, weakened, and empowered based upon what we look like.

Now isn't that just ducky?

I mean, aren't we just the most wonderful species ever? We have actually given the most power to the sense that, indeed, has the least amount of validity of them all!

Think about it; our eyes tell us who's pretty, ugly, fat, skinny, tall, short, black (even though no one is), white (again, no one is), and even go so far as to say who's good or bad based upon the way that they look. Which proves again a theory that one can indeed look with the eyes, but eyes are not required to "see", as I am again compelled to assert based on my acquaintance with those that have been, again, mislabeled "blind" who, in many ways, "see" better than most of us!

On the other hand the eyes are a most wonderful attribute of the human body. They allow us to identify, perceive, and observe. They show us what things look like and enable us to describe to others what something looks like. They enable us to perceive trees, the ocean, stars, birds and mountains. They allow us to perceive even each other and are indeed extremely helpful in our physical lives.

Magically and spiritually they are just the opposite, for we have a tendency to base our belief system on what things *look* like and not what they truly *are*. It is this folly that causes us to think that "looking" and "seeing" are the same. This is unfortunate as nothing could be further from the truth. Just because something looks a certain way doesn't make it so. But if we limit the sense of sight to the eyes, we are doomed to mistake the illusion of what something looks like for the reality of what can truly be called sight.

All in all the sense of sight can be a powerful tool, but is definitely NOT limited to the eyes...

AHURA Z. DILIIZA

4 THE ELEMENTS

The next phase of our adventure into the mystical will take us into an area that I am sure many of my colleagues will banter and debate about for many moons to come. We are now moving into the area of the elements...

The "elements" are the very forces of what everything is made up of. In other words, everything that there is on the face of the planet that we inhabit is made up of, powered by, sustained by and perpetuated by five basic elements.

Four of these elements are well-known and taught about frequently, however, because of my inherent pattern of making sure that there is no stone left unturned, I would ask you to indulge me as I repeat what you probably already know.

The four that you know are *fire, water, earth* and *air*. However the fifth is often misnamed and therefore misunderstood...

If you are going to practice any form of magic, mysticism, sorcery, alchemy, geomancy, vodoum ("voodoo", to the less informed), prayer, meditation or ceremony of any kind it is imperative that you learn how to form a healthy relationship with the elements. So, without further delay, let us begin...

Fire

Fire, being the most volatile of the elements, bids that we begin here. It is this element that is used in the representation of attributes such as passion, creativity, desire, action, drive, anger and war. Dedicated to the direction of the South and the color red, its nature is almost self-explanatory and its ability to command attention impeccable.

It can be both creative and destructive depending on how it is used. Its very presence demands respect and awe. Even in mythology the element of fire has been portrayed as the power that was given to man against the wishes of Zeus, King of the Gods.

This powerful element is the subject of many a verse in every holy book ever printed, sometimes as the very presence of God (as in the story of Moses) or as the holy flame of the Holy Spirit and sacred fire of magic. Fire has been used to inspire, to protect (as in forming a protective shield of fire) or even to instill fear and oppression (as in the pseudo-Christian depiction of Hell).

Fire is purifying and in its own way renewing, forgiving and obliterating. Absolutely savage and at the same time as perfectly refined. Where it passes there is always change and opportunity for growth. Beautiful and terrible would best describe the element that is called Fire.

Water

Equal to, and yet totally the opposite of fire is the element known as Water.

This element is the sustainer of all life on the planet and, quite possibly, the solar system. You will often find it as the representation of feeling, love, healing and growth. Its cleansing ability is almost miraculous and has, like fire, been the subject of many a philosophical, mystical and religious verse.

The direction attributed to water is the West, which is the direction of prosperity, growth, honesty, healing, empathy and telepathy. The color is blue. Even in mystical practices water is referred to as the great healer as there are ceremonies that can not only cleanse the body of sickness and dirt, but also cleanse the mind and etheric body of negative thought forms and karma.

Water is indeed the element of life, as without it everything that can be called alive would cease to exist...

Earth

Let is suffice to say that all of the elements that will be defined here are equal in magnitude and importance to life and existence, however I would like to draw your attention and interest to this particular element that is called Earth (or, as we that are mystically inclined like to refer to as "Mother Earth").

Ironically it is the one element that is most forgotten and taken for granted. Now before you deem it necessary to protest my seemingly accusatory gesticulation, think about it for just one moment and take into consideration the condition of the planet that we so blatantly rape and pillage for technology, science and "evolution" sake, and then remember that it is this very decimated LIVING element that we in our tangible state are comprised of.

Every mineral that is on the planet known as Earth (Gaia, Terra) is also within each one of us, which literally means that Mr. Einstein was right; we really are One...

You will find the earth represented in the attributes of strength, fertility, healing, growth, family, stability and foundation. Working in tandem with water it is the very womb and the resting place of all life.

No matter how great or small you are you will always return to the loving embrace of this element to be reborn to the reborn (and again be born) until which time that those who have created all things decide that you must needs be somewhere else (and even then it is one of her sisters that will give birth to you and again you will have this element within you).

All in all, the element Earth is the ultimate in support and substance. The direction of Earth is East, as it is the beginning and the freshness that can be called Life...

Wind/Air

Someone asked me once what the Holy Spirit felt like to me. I thought long and patiently and the answer came as easily as breathing; the wind (or air, for those of you who are sticklers for terminology).

The wind can shape the destiny of everyone at any given moment. It is the very breath that enables us to surmount our greatest difficulty. You will find the wind represented in the attributes of freedom, logic, evolution, intelligence, healing, speed and movement. It is the current of communication and the bed on which sound travels and rests.

If we use the element of air/wind to form our thoughts they will always lead us to the logical conclusion free from any influence other than pure intent and precision. It is this element that, in cooperation with water, not only reshapes us but indeed has the power to destroy, heal and make new everything.

The Wind or Air is truly (as all the elements are) Holy.

"The Fifth Element"...

OK, here we go. There has always been this HUGE mystique about what the much vaunted "fifth element" is...

Hollywood thinks that it is "Love" (as is portrayed in one of it's movies). The "airy-fairy" genre think it is "Akasha" (which even they don't understand!). And even still there are those who believe that it is "Spirit". They are indeed all good guesses (except for that last one; spirit is a principal, not an element – but then what do I know, right?).

The truth is that the "fifth element" is not as romantic as all that, and is again very important and essential to life as we know (and don't know) it. I think that once you find out what it is you will be "SHOCKED" at how obvious it should have been to you...

The fifth element is... electricity. Ha! How about that! Of all things, electricity!

Yes, that element that should be the most obvious, as without electricity there would be no magnetism. No magnetism, no gravity. No gravity and you wouldn't exist in a corporeal state and therefore not live.

Electricity runs through every element and is perpetuated by them all simultaneously. It is that which keeps us altogether, so to speak.

You will find electricity represented in the attributes of power, communication, warning, speed, protection, force, dynamic, judgment, rejuvenation, reincarnation and life.

Electricity is the all-pervading force of the God and Goddess that powers us all, whether we know it or not. Its direction is North, in the direction of power (and it is most definitely that...).

There you have it. The Elements. One does not govern the other and there is no way to separate them as they are in complete harmony with each other and work in oneness with each other (thankfully whether or not *we* work in oneness with each other). Throughout your education in Unicorn Magic you will endeavor to form and cultivate a relationship with them all as they have always been there within and without you, patiently awaiting your arrival at the doorway to magic and mysticism...

5 THE DIMENSIONS

Now that you have learned about the minds, the bodies, the senses and the elements it is time for you to learn about the first five of what are the dimensions, as it is these five that are the most important to you at this time. Throughout your lives you have often heard the term "dimension" and perhaps equated that term to the size, weight, depth, shape and height of a person, place or thing.

I'm going to use that education in order to draw you a picture of what the dimensions are. In order for me to do that I have to speak to you rather elementary, so please forgive me if I sound as if I think that you cannot comprehend simple physics. It is not my intention to insult.

The First Dimension

The first dimension can best be described as nothingness, like a blank screen that has no shape or form in any way. It has no top, bottom, left, right, up, down, in or out. It simply can only be described as "there".

The Second Dimension

The second dimension is just a little more interesting as it is a dimension that could be called linear. If you were to take a pen and draw a line on a piece of paper, perhaps even a circle, you would have an example of the second dimension.

That being said, I feel that it is important to understand that even though the second dimension is linear and the first is like a great nothingness they are alive. Remember that you exist in all of the dimensions that will be described, and that in order for you to live in them they must be alive, as only life can sustain life...

The Third Dimension

Interestingly enough it is the third dimension that we as human beings are the most familiar and comfortable with, as we are very sight-oriented and have difficulty in using anything other than our eyes to see with. However, in this case that could be a useful attribute.

The third dimension is the dimension of depth, height, width, weight, shape, color, size and placement. It is whether something is round or square, rough or smooth, tall or short etc. It is this dimension that dictates what can go in what space and how much can occupy a space at once.

For lack of a better term to describe the third let us call it the dimension of differentiation.

Now, in order for me to qualify the third dimension I have to quickly move on to the dimension that must be explained along with he third, and that would be...

The Fourth Dimension

The Fourth Dimension is the dimension of perception. In other words, it is how we know what is what and when is when, who is who, how it is, where it is, etc. (now you see why we have to introduce this dimension, as it is the one that allows me to describe the rest of them to you).

Without this dimension there would be no way to perceive anything, whether it was there or not. This dimension gives us the ability to send and receive sensory input and output however, unless it works with yet another dimension it is just like having a super computer with all the bells and whistles but without one vital component, and that would be...

The Fifth Dimension

The fifth dimension is the dimension of interaction. The place of reaction and response. It is the dimension that causes everything to move and stop, lift and drop, go in and out, around and around. It is the switch that turns all of the rides on at the carnival that we call life. Magnificent, isn't it? Just think of it; no matter how powerful a thing is, without the fifth dimension's influence in some way, shape or form it would be inert and therefore USELESS and might as well not exist.

The fifth has its mechanics in both life and death, as growth and decay are part of the same entity that is called the fifth dimension.

6 INTRODUCTION TO SPELLWORK

Now that you have received the explanations of the first five attributes that are the basic mechanics of the Universal practice that is Unicorn Light Mysticism, I would ask you to keep them in mind always as they will continue to serve throughout your education.   Remember, whether you practice the Sacred Magic of The Unicorn or any other type of magic, practicality should be ever present in your mind, heart and actions.   For in truth, if it cannot be applied practically it is NOT magic and therefore no good!

Now, before you receive your first spell let me caution you, the spells that have been constructed here are for use either:

- To bring about positive change
- To bring about Prosperity
- To ward off evil and psychic attack
- To heal yourself and others
- To bring love and peace to you and others
- To beautify
- To protect
- To increase your intelligence and help you to evolve

- To put you in touch with your highest good and increase your spiritual awareness
- To help you realize your totemic aspect and to help you find strength and beauty in your life

These spells may not be used to influence another being in any way, shape or form, nor may they be used to harm anyone at any time, under any circumstances.

I now, as your witness, decree that by the Power invested in me by the one true God and Goddess, and in the name and nature of the Christ Spirit I know as Jesus, I charge this book to return to the reader that which they sow, three times three times nine to thee.

So it is, so it is, so it is.

7 TOOLS AND SUPPLIES

Now, before we get started we are going to need some supplies. These can be either created or purchased almost anywhere. I personally prefer to create my tools as it affords me the assurance that it is my thought, and my thought alone that went into the creation of the tool, and my thought and energy that will permeate my action. I will explain: In the beginning chapters of this book I gave a brief synopsis of the etheric, or ethereal body. Within this body is the energetic body which is involved in every aspect of the Universe. No matter how great or small, the great equalizer is energy.

You see, in the beginning there was only energy. Even the very creators of the Universe released this to us in our earlier development as part of our evolution as spiritual beings. The duality of good and evil did not exist, and there was only one which expressed itself in many forms, yet none of them dissonant. As a result of certain events (which I will gingerly step over and address in advanced lessons) energy became split--and directed into the split--and thus duality was born. These concepts later took on lives and identities of their own and, like all things that live, it seeks only to promote its existence. It will enlist the help of anyone capable of directing it. In other words, it is WE that are responsible for the life and growth of energy just as it is responsible for us. Odd isn't it? The very thing that makes up the Universe is also what we are made of. Based upon that particular premise, that means that *we* to some degree have the ability to manifest ourselves, using ourselves to do it.

Taking this into consideration, once we have made a decision as to what our alignment is, energy makes itself available to us. Whether we choose to use this energy for good or bad has absolutely nothing to do with energy itself. In fact, this a decision that rests solely with us. Whatever your alignment is, energy will provide. It is this which also enables us to form energy into what we call *magic*, or the art of manifesting what we need in our lives from seemingly nothing.

There are thousands of different types of energy (and no, there is no way to count them all as they are ever changing and evolving). These energies combine in order to create and take the shape of whatever is needed or imagined. The earth, the sun, stars and moon are all a part of what energy has combined to create. — Forgive me if every once in awhile I lean toward the "scientific", but it is in this area that a very well known scientist (that we shall, for the sake of prudence, refer to as "Mr. H.") and myself meet and agree — Because of the boundless amount of energy that flows throughout the universe the potential for creativity is unfathomable.

Now let us bring this home by relating it to ourselves: We need something to happen in our lives, and to make these things happen we need to employ a small fraction of this powerful force that we call "energy" in order to accomplish our goal. Pretty simple so far, yes? Good. First we need something to capture and shape energy with. Fortunately, that particular tool is already within us. That tool is your mind. You see, there is some truth to the saying "where your thoughts go your energy flows".

You use your mind to gather energy by thinking of the thing that you need or want to happen. For instance, you need a new job. The obvious states that you need to look for one. However, the not-so-obvious says that you need to use that magnificent tool that we call *mind* to envision, or "visualize" your participation in that very thing that we want to happen (I must emphasize *participation* for it is YOU that is the focus of what you need to happen, and therefore YOU that must be both visualizer and vision). It is at this point that the great forces of energy will focus themselves on you – *both* of you. The combination of energies both tangible (you the *seer*) and intangible (you the *vision*) causes an actual divine principal to leap into action (okay, perhaps the word "leap" is a bit sensational, but all the same this principal activates).

That principal? Easy. 1+1=3.

Not so easy you say? Well, let's see (*author inhales deeply*)...

Throughout all time, those that know the nature of manifestation know this: Energy, in it's ever expanding nature is to be used for two things, either for creation or procreation. Either way there must be two different elements in order to cause the great manifestation machine to work. That machine creates a third energy that is a mixture of both involved. What this means is (for those of you who missed that class which was supposed to take the place of the parental "birds and bees" speech), when you take the intimate energy of a man, and place it with the intimate energy of a woman, under the right conditions you get a child. This child is a combination of both beings involved. A hybrid if you will, carrying the energy and vital traits of both, yet living and breathing on its own, growing stronger with each passing moment. This is called *procreation*.

The same thing happens with energy. The tangible blends with the intangible causing a third energy to emerge. This new hybrid lives and breathes a combination of both *you* and *you*. It is the shining example of the union between you the seer and you the vision. This is called *creation*.

So, what have we learned? That it takes two physical beings combining physical energy to create a child (procreation). Likewise, it takes a *seer* and a *vision* – or the combination of tangible and intangible energy – to create. And thus, *one plus one equals three* (whew!).

Please forgive my lengthy explanation but it is the only way to paint you a picture of your most valuable and important tool in mysticism and magic. Your MIND.

The second thing that you will need is *representation*.

What exactly do I mean by representation? Again we must refer to the earlier lesson of the elements. You will need a representative of all of them.

Here are some good ideas for representation...

Fire

A candle holder and plenty of candles. I prefer white, unscented candles as the lack of color or scent usually suggests that there has not yet been an intention placed on them. I know that in many schools of thought on magic there are a multitude of colors used in ceremonial magic, suggesting that the color of the candle will invoke the attribute assigned to that color. As a practitioner and teacher of the art of Vibrational Frequency, though I agree that color can be used in manifestation because of the different vibratory ratios assigned to certain attributes, the point of using the candle in the first place is for the element of fire which always, no matter what color candle you use, burns the same color, and that is the color of... FIRE!

Water

A shell, glass, stone, metal, or crystal bowl will do. Water is an element that will take the shape of whatever you place it in. If you honor it, like all elements it will honor you. If you must place it in a metal receptacle I prefer silver as it reflects the very nature of water; the Goddess force, the life giver, and the moon. You will use water to cleanse, bathe, meditate and drink. You, with your thought, will magnetize the water to conduct your thought and energy, and it will flow through you creating and maintaining you so that you can grow to understand that water is you, and you are it. So to honor yourself is to honor WATER...

Wind/Air

A feather, ribbon, windmill, or sheer cloth that flows easily. It is highly recommended that when you endeavor to perform an act of mysticism that you allow even your hair to flow freely, as the wind will not cooperate if you become an obstacle to it. What I mean by this is that the wind is the very breath of life. That life needs to flow. When you cooperate with the wind by offering it something that it can dance with, such as flowing cloth, garments, or even your hair, you have actually invited the wind to live with you, and accept you into its world. Once you have invited it to come and play, you must take care not to show it anything that would suggest that you want to imprison or interfere with it in any way, as it will retreat from you like a threatened bird. Remember this and choose your invitations carefully. The relationship between the wind and you must ALWAYS be one of respect and cooperation. You must always remember the wind in your ceremony as it constantly remembers you, so make your representation of it WONDERFUL, and your results will happen in kind.

Earth

A stone will do as it is the most uncomplicated element of all. I assign my students to find twelve white stones. The twelve white stones represent the twelve tribes of our particular solar system. Each tribe is assigned an Earth, or planet as we call them. This suggests that there was at some point 12 Earths, or planets in our solar system. The twelve tribes belong to 12 kingdoms, under the sun. Those 12 kingdoms later became known to us as astrological signs, represented by 12 symbols, or creatures. These creatures, although quite mythical in appearance represented the outstanding attributes of each tribe. Each of these representations bear with them a stone that has certain "mystical" properties that can influence elements on our earth and other planets. The one quality that each of the planets have is that they all have stone. It is this which allows us to call upon all of them as it is our earth that is made up of each of them hence the need for stones. To have twelve stones is to have twelve planets.

A staff or wooden wand, as wood symbolizes life on this particular planet. Of all living things it is the trees that have witnessed the growth and expansion of the Great Mother. Like silent sentinels, they help divinity create life giving air by transforming used, or even toxic elements into clean oxygenated energy. The tree, or staff should be crafted by you but if there is someone that you hold confidence in then so be it. The staff will be a point of focus for your ceremonies and rituals so choose your wood carefully. If you find a worthy piece of wood, please respect the tree that it came from, and give an offering as soon as possible.

So, based upon this explanation you should be able to see why EARTH is properly represented by a simple stone, or staff.

Lightening/Electricity

A silver rod, or wand will suffice. Now, I know that the initial reaction will be to go and look for a beautiful bejeweled wand of sterling silver that glows in the night like Sir Lancelot's lance, but I assure you this is not necessary.

Go to the nearest jewelry supply shop and purchase a piece of silver wire, about 1/4 inch thick, and 12 inches long. Sharpen both ends to a sharp point. Now, I know that most of us are quite careful, but for those of us that feel the strong urge to run with pointy objects (probably because of some past life memory episode), I must remind you to please be careful. You are crafting something that is a representative of LIGHTNING. Caution must be observed.

Sand the rod to smoothness and polish it to its brightest. This next step is very important: The next time there is a storm, place the rod outside or in a window so that it will absorb the energy from the lightning of the storm. Once again I must caution you; lightning is extremely volatile and nothing to be taken "light"-ly. Please do not walk out into a dangerous storm believing something that you may have seen in a comic book. (If I am so adamant about this point, it should be obvious that I have had the experience of stopping a person from standing in a lightning storm with a silver rod. I blame too much T.V. as this person believed that he was an immortal, and that he was the only "The One" that there could be). Remember: Lightning is the fifth element, and doesn't like repeating itself.

After retrieving your rod, place it in a soft cloth and allow NO ONE other than yourself to touch it. You have completed your representation, and are ready to greet LIGHTNING...

Daggers

Now that you have all of the elements properly represented, we are ready to move on to the next tool that you will need –

daggers. (Personally I prefer to call them daggers only because the word *athame* means very little to me. However "dagger", "knife", or "cutting tool" does). You will need two. One is for cutting and harvesting herbs (this dagger usually has a dark colored handle to signify that it is utilitarian) and one for ceremonial purposes (this one usually has a light colored handle). This dagger should be carefully picked and prepared as it will be the instrument that you wield as a magnet for mystical energy as you perform such incantations that I will provide you with. You will use this dagger to bring to a point the energy that is needed to manifest your desire (there are those that use a sword depending on the spell, but in most cases the dagger, or "athame" will suffice).

Altar

The altar is a special place in your home that no one but you may approach. It is where you keep your sacred objects. It is a good practice to keep your altar covered or closed away if you have guests, unless the guests are of like mind. The reason for this is to keep the thought of your altar untainted by judgment,or errant hands that seem to leap away from their owner to touch things that do not belong to them. Your altar is where you will perform most of your ceremonies and meditations. Some of the afore-mentioned tools will be kept there along with a bell to shatter any unwanted vibration. Your candle holder, water bowl, dagger and elemental objects may be kept there as well. In my home the altar is in a place that is obviously off limits to guests. If anyone ventures into the area, I politely tell them that it is off limits. If they ask why, I tell them (smiling), "Because I said so". When you are practicing you must never apologize for the rules in your home, especially when it comes to sacred objects. Your altar is a power station for you, and should be regarded as such and protected.

Get a small shelf or table. If you have the talent to build one, WONDERFUL! Have at you. If you are not suited in this area, your local shopping facility is sure to have the perfect thing (remember, the best is seldom defined by the expense, so use common sense). Take your shelf and clean it.

You might ask; *"But Mr. Unicorn Magic-teacher-person, what if the table/shelf is fresh out of the box?"*

And I might answer: Well Unicorn Magic-learning-person, as I mentioned before, you want your tools to completely have your energy, and by cleaning the table, you are wiping away the residual energy of the persons that built the table. Maybe when the person was building he was having a bad day and unconsciously projected his frustration onto your table (now, while this is most likely NOT the case, when it comes to preparing your altar it is best to eliminate the potential).

Once your table is cleaned find a nice cloth to put on it. The cloth can be anything that you like, as long as it shows your reverence and respect of the craft that you are endeavoring to master. I will make some suggestions if you will indulge me:

Silk. Because of the special texture of the material, it has long been established by the mystic world that this material is among the purest that there is (ironic that it is spun from the cocoon of worms...). Silk has the uncanny ability to actually block errant thought. (Imagine; you would THINK that we'd all wear this mystical material and be free of most psychic attacks, but this is a discussion for another time...). Silk. A worthy altar material.

Satin. Indeed a beautiful choice as it adds richness and opulence to any setting. Though the attribute of satin is more intimate than mystical, it too is worthy for your altar cloth.

Cotton, linen, canvas. If you want your altar to reflect the discipline of the art that you are learning, there are no better materials than these three. The simple integrity of these three materials bear with them a cleanliness that can remind one of childhood. If you just take a moment when you pick up a piece of linen you can almost hear the material sing of magic and adventure. Cotton always smells of fresh air, and canvas seems to assure you that it will not tear, thus giving strength to however it is used.

Take a moment before picking. There are those that would pick because of the popular opinion, but I must caution you that popular does not mean right. We are all different from one another, and should therefore never do something because someone else did. Even identical twins are different and therefore, in and of themselves unique. That being said let your choice, like yourself be unique.

Spread your new cloth evenly over your new table, and recite these words.

> *I place my altar cloth and stand*
> *to be touched only by my hand,*
> *and by my breath serve only me,*
> *as my kiss lands so shall it be...*

Lift your hand to your mouth and kiss your first two fingers (these two fingers represent power and glory, or conviction, and by kissing them you are invoking these principals). Blow on your fingers and then place them in the middle of the clothed table. You have in essence given your altar life. This action begins an intimate relationship between you and you altar, which is an instrument of the craft that you are learning. As all marriages take place upon an altar, so then does this one. You and your altar are one.

Place your candle holder and water bowl next to each other, and then your bell. Your representations of the elements are to be placed at the edges in a pyramid formation, beginning at 4:00 with Earth, going clockwise to Air/Wind, at 8:00. End your formation at 12:00 with LIGHTNING. Place an incense holder in the middle with fire and water, light a candle and sit quietly reflecting upon what you have accomplished. You are now ready to begin. Your altar is ready.

Lighter/Matches

There are many ways to light your candles, and I have been witness to many a heated debate on whether it is better to use matches or a lighter (silly argument really if you think about the desired result; fire gets to be either way). If you prefer the ambiance of striking a match to light your candles, then let no one speak against you. If the spark of the flint appeals more to your liking then flick your flint and blessed be, for both will do what is needed.

Herbs

A healthy supply of herbs are essential to the practice of mysticism. There are teas, infusions, tinctures, ointments, balms, and brews that will become an everyday part of your practice. I will give you a brief list of herbs to get you started...

Allspice	Chamomile
Ginseng	Anise
Cinnamon	Hyssop
Arrowroot	Clover
Lavender	Ash
Cloves	Lilac
Astragalus	Cramp bark
Malva	Balm of Gilead
Damiana	Mullein
Balsam	Dragon's blood
Nettle	Basil
Dandelion	Parsley
Banana leaf (really, it's an herb)	Dill
Rose hips and petals	Bee balm

Dongquai   Spearmint
Benzoin   Echinacea
Thyme   Blessed Thistle
Evergreen   Valerian
Calamus   Ginger
White Willow

Most herbs can be categorized into groups. Herbs such as Arrowroot, Astragalus, Balm of Gilead, Chamomile, Clove, Cramp Bark, Dongquai, Echinacea, Mullein, Valerian, and White Willow can be termed as medicinal.

Herbs such as Bee Balm, Benzoin, Blessed Thistle, Cinnamon, Dragon's Blood, Lavender, Lilac and Rose hips can be used for divining and meditational purposes.

Herbs such as Allspice, Anise, Basil, Clover, Dill, Ginger, Nettle, Parsley, and Thyme are mostly used for culinary purposes.

This brief categorization is not to be taken literally. The herbs that you see listed here can be cross used at any time. For instance. If you want to create the perfect meditational brew to calm the body and open the higher centers of the conscious mind, take a pinch of spearmint, add a pinch of lavender, jasmine and cinnamon. Mix them into one fifth cup of black tea. Stir the mixture well with a clean silver spoon, and you have a perfect dry mixture. One fourth teaspoon will make a fine tea that will place you in a perfect state for meditation.

Some herbs can be used for ceremony and healing practices but may not be ingested (we will cover this in our next issue as this is an introduction into the wonderful world of Unicorn Light Mysticism).

Medicinal mixtures take an advanced understanding of herbal properties and chemical components. Some of them can be dangerous and, while the practice of herbalism demands that eventually I release to you what I know of medicinal herbs, the responsible instructor in me chooses to wait until I know that we are ready for such things. I have had occasion to deal with individuals who after viewing a movie or popular T.V. show, decided that they should delve into the wonderful world of herbal compounds, and mixtures. Uneducated these individuals believed that it was a GOOD idea to make a mixture of herbs that are known to be hallucinogenic, and even poisonous, and smoke them. So I will allow the reader to mature in the use of herbs before we journey into the medicinal.

Herbalism is a part of Unicorn Light Mysticism that you will enjoy and benefit from so long as you are responsible and respectful of nature and humanity.

All in all, these are basic tools that you will need to begin.

AHURA Z. DILIIZA

8 BEGINNING SPELLWORK

Let's start with something simple. Years ago I learned a simple spell (that was more of an affirmation actually). The spell/meditation was given to me by my teacher, a very powerful mystic that I shall, for prudence sake, refer to simply as *Sri*.

Sit, or stand comfortably. Calm yourself. Take a deep breath. Exhale and take another deep breath. As you take one more breath, visualize everything that has caused you stress or imbalance, everything that has told you that you are not a wholly spiritual being. Take these things in the palm of your hand in your minds eye. Exhale slowly, and blow them all away...

Repeat this twice more, and those things that have plagued you should leave you.

Although I have re-created this spell so that it suits my particular method, the basic construct is the same as when my teacher taught it to me. It is my hope that you will do the same once you have mastered the method handed to you; you will re create it to fit your style and energy (don't worry, if you remain true to the principal of this exercise then you will perform it correctly, no matter how it is delivered. Master and then enhance. THAT is the way of the Mystic...).

Spells should never be complicated. If your spell is complicated your energy goes too much into the steps and not the goal. An incantation or spell should be easy to learn, practice and master. For instance; draw a simple pyramid and a lightning bolt that appears to go in one side and out the other.
It may be drawn on a piece of paper and placed on the wall, or even on the floor or ground where you live. As you place this paper (or as you scrawl it on the floor) recite these words:

Sacred symbol I now I charge thee,
From all forms of evil do protect me.
My family and myself be free,
So Goddess wills, so it shall be.

That simple. You will find that no matter what kind of spell you endeavor to perform, the simplest spells are the most powerful.

There are three basic types of spells:

- Those that operate during the waxing moon.
- Those that operate during the waning moon.
- Those that operate transcending phases of the moon.

This will be very important as the moon will become a powerful ally in your mystical development and your spell work. Remember, the spell should always fit the need – and there should ALWAYS be a legitimate need. Magic is not a toy, or joke, and should be approached with reverence and respect.

Now, it has been my experience, that most people seek help in the areas of

- Prosperity
- Protection
- Healing
- Vision
- Love

Therefore, it is in these areas that we will concentrate our lesson. First, let us address the area of prosperity...

AHURA Z. DILIIZA

9 PROSPERITY SPELL

When we think of prosperity more often than not the image that is associated with the word is money. While the term has many actual images and references, I think that we can agree unanimously that the strongest is money so it is here that we will focus our attention.

The spell that I will give you will allow you to step into the very place that all prosperity comes from. The whole idea is to help you participate in the manifestation of your financial well being. We all have had to deal with money problems and many of us have said that if we could do something about it we would. While common sense is always paramount even in the practice of mysticism, we must consider those things that would cause one to exercise faith. It is this that we will do by performing this spell.

We shall call upon the power of the elements themselves to deliver to us the energy of prosperity that will help us to fulfill our monetary needs. We must first turn to the *waxing moon* as all spells that deliver to us what we need is a polarity of attraction, or bringing something to us ("waxing" means the increasing visibility of the moon as it moves towards full). Likewise, if we want something to leave us we must employ the *waning* or shrinking moon (what this means is that the moon is slowly becoming less visible as it reaches what is called the "new moon").

Get a silver coin, a coin that is legal tender in the country that you live in. It is prosperity that you asking for, money specifically, so your coin should be in the currency of the country that you live in. It would do you no good to live in America, yet have as your representation a Canadian quarter as you would not be able to spend it in America, and may in fact manifest Canadian money (which may work for certain places in Maine, but not for the rest of the country...).

Gather your wits, and clear your mind. Place yourself comfortably and light your candle (again white, unscented). If you feel strongly about using the color green then wear something green, as your idea of prosperity will indeed help you, so long as it is real to you (and clothing is real enough to all of us). Hold the coin in your dominant hand, as this is the hand that is known as your *power* or *force* hand. Think of how much you need to manifest, and see yourself doing what needs to be done with the money that the Universe has provided you with.

Blow on your hand three times, and recite these words:

> *Earth, fire, wind, and sea,*
> *Grant your power invest in me.*
> *One in three is three in one,*
> *Prosperity's show has now begun,*
> *To us, to us, in God we trust,*
> *Affluence now is finding us.*
> *Money comes in three times three,*
> *As nature moves so shall it be!*

Repeat this seven times, and know that your spell has worked.

Sit for a moment and ponder what you have done. Never discuss your spell with anyone else, as you must protect the vision of what you need to manifest until its fruition. *Cast not your pearls before swine* as my role model, Jesus would say – which brings me to an important bit of information that I personally wish to share...

In many instances throughout this class I will make reference to God, Goddess, Jesus, Krishna, Athena, Buddha, and other beings that are known well in the religious world. The Christ I know as Jesus has and will ALWAYS be my role model, and example of the perfect Mystic. Although I am certain to offend some religious groups, I might remind the more learned in these groups that the Unicorn was at one time the symbol of Christ. The way I see it, Jesus was a Unicorn... That being said I respect all beliefs so long as they promote positivity and peace. I serve the Goddess nature, and will confidently and proudly speak of her often.

Now, on to the next spell...

AHURA Z. DILIIZA

10 CALLING THE WIND

Light your candle and set your staff next to you, for we are going to make a request of the wind.

"Excuse me Mr. Unicorn, um did you say the wind? So why do I need a staff?"

Great question. Remember when I said that all of the elements work together? Well this is one of those times when you get to be a witness to the cooperation between them. One of the best ways to see this interaction is with the ancient art of Tai Chi.

As I performed a movement called *Raising The Wind* I observed something wonderful...

As the wind approached, the giant Gingko tree that I was practicing under began to sing. The leaves rustled with the presence of the wind from the very direction that I was raising it from. Now, now, for all of you that would say, *"But what's so magical about the wind blowing through the trees, it happens all the time?"*. While this is true, I would say to you that before I performed this movement:

- The wind was not moving at the velocity that it was until I called for it.
- It was in fact blowing in a different direction before I called.
- The Gingko tree did not move with the wind until after I called.
- The rustle of the leaves was so pronounced that even people walking by stopped to look, as that particular day was hot, humid and still.
- I needed the wind. I called. She came, and made the tree sing. It helped all around, and I got to witness how the tree heralded the coming of the wind, so this is the reason for the use of a staff when performing this wind spell.

For those of you that are NOT psychic or telepathic the staff will serve as a way for you to actually feel when the energy of the wind is approaching for your spell. Remember your basic lessons in science: energy always precedes matter, and although the wind is not detectable until it chooses to be, it is nevertheless a form of matter, so your staff will serve.

Now, we must decide the direction that we will request the wind to come from. Each direction bares with is basic principals and spiritual energies. While the wind is perfect unity it is also universal, which means that it has direction and therefore needs be addressed directly and specifically.

These are the attributes of the wind:

North

Archangel Michael. Winter, protection, power, purity, banishment, death, and reincarnation, black.

South

Archangel Uriel. Summer, strength, speed, guardianship, literary skill, removal of obstacles, endurance, red.

East

Archangel Raphael. Spring, beginnings, youth, rejuvenation, knowledge, agreement white/yellow.

West

Archangel Gabriel. Fall, love, healing, prosperity, music, beauty, life, fertility, blue/green.

(Of course each direction has many other attributes, but for this lesson the ones that I have named will suffice.)

Now that we have a basic knowledge of direction and the attributes of each, lets choose.

Since we are in the sector of prosperity let us make a request of the West wind.

Turn to the left, hold your hands palm up. Pull them close to your body, just beneath your solar plexus. Envision that which you need to happen, close your eyes, and recite these words:

> *Sacred West Wind hear my plight,*
> *I ask of you your help this night.*
> *Upon your breath I bid you bring*
> *The gold I need to make me sing.*
> *My needs fulfilled I tap my tree,*
> *Three times, and leave this task to thee!*

Now lift your staff and tap it three times on the floor or ground and wait silently. Do not move for it is vigilance that the wind looks for. The West Wind is much like a lover. To advance, move, or leave before the West Wind is ready for you to would effectively (ahem) "spoil the mood" and she would retreat from you, and the next time you would have much difficulty capturing her attention.

You will hear a sound much like a small bell, and then a soft breeze will caress your cheek. It is then and only then that you may stand. Bow, thank the West Wind, and back away from the place that you have made your request (if you've paid attention to your earlier lesson of how to regard your altar, you will understand why it is proper to back away as opposed to turning your back. The earth is the altar of the wind, and the wind is the protector of the earth, so please, respect is in order).

Mysticism in its finest form, as I said earlier, is always in its *simplest* form. Another term for simple in the mind of the earnest practitioner is "practical". Practicality is that which keeps us grounded or sane. Mysticism, or magic, is an essential part of the existence of humankind (although the scientific community might disagree, without the many aspects of early mysticism, science itself would not exist).

Take for example astronomy. Without the earlier practice of astrology, there would be no astronomy. Both are based upon mathematics and physical celestial logistics. The greater form of celestial/physical logistics, or mechanics, is called *quantum physics* (which every quantum physician MUST, even against their own stubborn will, admit is merely "possibility" – even probability – and therefore falls under the auspices of *metaphysics,* the very mother of mysticism).

The scientist seeks to prove or disprove. The metaphysician seeks to realize and manifest.
Hmm... not so far apart are we?

Getting back to practicality: Fairly, on the side of science you could very well be able to manifest a fireball in your hand, but what good is it if you and your family are impoverished or hungry? Therefore practical mysticism deems that I teach you something that will indeed help.

AHURA Z. DILIIZA

11 MAGIC CEREAL

This one has specifically to do with food and confidence. I know that you will enjoy it...

Years ago, a young boy was having trouble in school. No matter how hard he tried he just could not keep up with what was expected of him in his classes. I knew the boy, and his history. Because of epileptic seizures (as the result of an injury he suffered when he was younger) he was placed on a very powerful medication which slowed his thinking process significantly. Day after day this child would endure countless taunts from the other children, desperately fighting for the opportunity to prove that he was not what they labeled him (those who have ever suffered at the hands or words of a bully know the names well so I do not think its necessary to speak or write them). His confidence was nearly destroyed.

Finally, his mother asked if there was anything that I could do. I looked at the young boy,
and as he looked up at me I saw in his eyes a look that I never wish to see again in my life. I saw pure desperation. I saw the dejection that a person has when they believe that all hope is lost. It was as if someone took him like an old rag and squeezed every bit of confidence out of him. He blinked and lowered his head.

I went to him and said, "Hard time huh?"

Without looking back he said, "I- I'm stupid".

I felt as if someone had just hit me in the chest with a sledge hammer. I visibly flinched and shook my head as a fighter would to shake off the effects of a hard punch.

"No son. No you're not. You just need a little help that's all".

"But I always get it wrong! It's like my- my head wont work. I get mad because the other kids make fun of me, and the teacher sends ME to the office because I yell at them, but I cant help it".

By then he was choking on his words, tears streaming down his face.

"I see...". I mused. "Let's try something. I think that I can make you smarter".

He quickly turned his head toward me. "What?"

"I think I can make you smarter. You know, get everything right?" I dramatically tapped my finger on the side of my head, and then pointed at an imaginary object in the air. "Yes, yes I'm sure of it!". *Ha HAH! I have his attention* I thought. He'd stopped crying, and was doing that funny little inhale-hiccup thingy that kids do.

"Y- (*hic*) you ca- (*hic*) can?"

"Yes I can".

I told him about something that I made once that was called "Magic Cereal" and that it operated only for the children that thought it tasted good, because if they liked it, they would get smarter and pass AAALLL of their tests. His face brightened dramatically. His eyes searched the air as if looking for something and then....

"HEY! I got it!" he yelped.

The sad face totally changed. He was the very picture of excitement!

"What?" I said.

"What if you made magic cereal, and I liked it. Would it work on me?"

"Hmm. I don't know. We could give it a shot if you think it's a good idea".

"AWESOME!"

Before I could say anything else the boy ran over to his mother and asked if "Z" could make magic cereal. She smiled to see him so excited, and said "Oh my, magic cereal is it? Okay". The boy yelled and wanted to go to the store immediately to get the ingredients.

This recipe is very sweet, and uses lots of sugar sooo...

For parents that do not allow their children to eat sugar there are ways to adapt the recipe to not-fun-at-all (but this is supposed to be about the child, not you!). For those of you who are diabetic, please consult your physician before attempting this recipe (while this is called Magic Cereal, it is not excuse to act irresponsibly).

For those of you who have begged me for the recipe, here it is...

You will need:

- A white unscented candle
- Banana or apple (fresh) 1 whole
- Ground cinnamon, 1 tsp
- Sunflower seeds (unsalted)
- Sugar, 1/4 cup
- Molasses, 3 teaspoons
- Brown sugar, 1/2 cup
- Dates, chopped (to your standard)
- Raisins, 1/4 cup
- Butter or margarine(unsalted) 1/4 stick
- Oats, 1 cup
- Grits, 2 cups
- A pot (to suit)
- A wooden spoon (works best for magic)

Light your safely placed candle. Take a small pinch of cinnamon. Go to the candle, bow and say:

> *Southern Wind assist my feat,*
> *For magic, I require your heat.*
> *This pleasant scent I offer you,*
> *And consecrate my magic brew.*

Sprinkle the cinnamon lightly onto the flame (please be careful), and let the smoke from the cinnamon lift into the air. Take your pot of water, and set it on the burner. When the water comes to boil, add your cinnamon and oats. Add the grits, along with the apples (if that is your desired fruit). Next put your brown sugar and white sugar in.

Turn the heat down to allow everything to simmer. Stirring constantly, add the raisins and dates. Stir in your molasses. A magnificent scent should fill your home. The scent should bring the sense of well being and comfort. After the oats are done to your desire, turn off your heat. Thank the South Wind, and finally add your sunflower seeds. The finishing touches are the butter and honey. Take a small portion for yourself and test it. A bit of butter and a light drizzle of honey and we are complete.

Call the nearest child (whether they are 2 or 92!). Tell them that this is Magic Cereal, and if they like it they will get everything right today. Speak slowly, and dramatically so that they get the full impact of your power, smiling beatifically, knowing that you are successful in your task.

The child or person that you give it to will smile, and you will see what I saw so many years ago, just before the boy finished every bit of the Magic Cereal, grabbed his bag and hurried off to school knowing that everything would be fine.

Remember: Magic is also confidence, which merely had to be restored to the child using a method that the child found pleasing. I only gave the boy a way back to the place that magic exists bountifully; childhood.

Oh yes. Later that afternoon the boy ran home waving a math test high in the air

like a triumphant Olympian raising the flag of his country after winning the gold medal.

"I-GOT-AN-AAAA" he shrieked "I did it!!! I did it!!!", waving his paper (shortly after that he began to perform a song dance that made me wonder if maybe I should call it alien   cereal...).   "I   did   it,   I   did   it, IATETHEMAGICCEREALANDTHENIGOTITRIIIIIIIII IGHT! YEAH!!" (no kidding this is exactly the way it sounded).

He showed me the paper and to my immediate pleasure, above twelve math questions was a glowing red "A" and a happy face. The boy gave me a big hug and said "thank you", to which I could only say, "Well done young man". The magic cereal worked.

The next day at about 7:30 in the morning there was a knock at my front door. I opened the door and there were four children gazing at me smiling...

"Hi", I said.

"Can we have some Magic Cereal??"

By the end of the week there were 15 children and two parents sitting at my breakfast table, and each of them had success stories to tell as a result of eating Magic Cereal. So at the request of my students (all ADULT children!) the recipe is finally released. Magic Cereal is for *everyone* as were all someone's child, and need only remember the magic that is always available to us.

One more thing. That young boy? Last I heard he was in college and doing very well. And yes, he still remembers "Magic Cereal".

Enjoy!

THE WAY OF THE UNICORN

12 MATCHLESS

The next segment of this lesson has to do with the mind. The part of the mind which has to do with mental speed to be exact. While I am sure that this begs the question. *But what does mental speed have to do with magic?* Simple. In order to be effective in our everyday existence (notwithstanding in the halls of mysticism) we must be able to focus clearly and concentrate thought in spite of the constant noise and confusion that surrounds us.

Everything that could possibly be a distraction seems to decide, at the very moment that you need to focus, to amplify itself as if on cue. You get a precious few moments to meditate. You set up your circle, light your candles and incense, turn on your favorite mood music, sit in the required position and begin. You breathe deeply and clear your mind. *Clear your miiinnd. Clleeeaarr yourr mmiiiiinnnddd...* Suddenly, just as you begin to feel the celestial presence of your inner being, someone decides that it's a great idea to test how well their high-powered motorcycle engine works. No worries. You have honed your mental capacity to just about ignore the rolling thunder.

Just as it dissipates, the neighbors dog spots the local stray cat, which has discovered that the dog cannot reach it, and instead of mercifully running and hiding so that you can resume your communion in peace, the contentious kitty struts its feline stuff slowly as if saying, *Hah! Silly dog. Don't you know that there is a person trying to meditate?* As you reinforce your concentration to ignore the *yap-yap-yap* of the little animal an itch makes itself present. The itch is small, and you know it will go away so you proceed. However the stupid dog is still barking, that moron with the motorcycle is going the opposite direction, and the darn itch isn't going away. You (against your will) start to entertain the idea of scratching the itch, but that would probably make it worse. The dog needs to have its face duck-taped. Is it called duck tape? What a funny name. Oh, it's *duct* tape. Well fine *duct* tape the little rat-dog. And will SOMEbody please show that IDIOT which direction he needs to go so that he stops going back and forth as if EVERYone in the neighborhood bought their house SOLE-ly so that we could listen to his STOOPID MOTOR BIKE?!!

Suddenly, as if your guides have responded to your request, the dog has quit its yapping, and the motorcycle has found its direction and gone. The itch has abated and peace has again found you. You take a deep breath, and relax...

Then, it happens: the doorbell rings. Its your brother come to visit. Your eyes snap open
and you lose it. "Really? *REALLY???*" The moment is shattered. You get up and decide that you will try another time.

I am certain we have all seen particular episode of life on Earth however, there is hope. With the incantation that I'm about to give you, you will be able to not only speed up your mental processing capability, you will also open the portion of your mind that deals with intuition. Remember a basic universal mechanic: the faster the vibratory rate, the higher the vibrational energy. The higher the vibrational energy, the greater the potential for the distribution of said energy, which means the greater the potential to see and effect change within the three states of reality (the past, the future, and the *now*).

Excuse me Mr. Unicorn-magic-guy. What do you mean by the NOW?

The *now* is where the future and past meet. I will explain the full breadth of exactly what the *now* is as I have been taught and have grown to understand in later lessons, but as for now let it suffice to say that all that you have ever been and will be exists to some extent "now". It is a great juxtaposition of all linear time and space as we know it. Let us return to our lesson...

One of the benefits of increased vibrational speed is increased energy, mental and even physical speed. You will employ an incantation which, by constant repetition and reinforcement, will become the vehicle that you will use to focus your concentrated thought-energy in order to accelerate your vibrational frequency. With this technique even certain aspects of the physical metabolic rate can be increased along with an increase of the vibrational frequency.

Your work, relationships, and the power to manifest that which you need in your life can be enhanced. Your ability to focus and concentrate will increase almost instantaneously.

Pretty cool huh? With an increase of your mental ability you will no longer be plagued by those things that would normally distract you, and you will succeed in your efforts to reach your perfect space.

So, for the sake of staying (somewhat) within the bounds of simplicity, here is the incantation.

Light your candle and sit or stand comfortably. Use your staff, foot or hand to tap a soft but steady rhythm and recite these words:

Matchless is my speed of mind
I shall leave my past behind
Further, further from my thoughts
Are those things which come to naught
Fire, fire burn my foes
'Till they loose me from my woes
From all danger set me free
Only peace resides in me!

Start a regiment of saying this ten times a day (if you find your beat and want to do more
who am I to stand in the way of enthusiasm?). Within three days you should see results.

It doesn't seem possible that a few words said in a rhythmic pattern could affect the way that I think, or speed up my thinking process. I'm sorry Mr. Unicorn, but you're asking me to believe something that has not been scientifically proven.

Well I might remind you that science is only capable of giving a theory on that which we already know such as "water is wet" or "if you fall asleep under a tree heavy laden with ripe apples, you are more than likely going to get hit in the head". What most in these modern times call science is really opportunistic disregard for the purity that was once called science in order to make money and satisfy the individualist ego. The pure scientist understands that one must always consider that the tree falling in the forest still makes a sound whether or not you are there to hear it. Science – ALL science – is truly the offspring of the great mother of all abilities. That mothers name is ART and the firstborn was mysticism.

While I will not drop cotton balls through a doorway and try to catch them with psychic ability, or guess what's in an envelope for a million dollars, I WILL stand by the practice of mysticism and remind all that the intelligence and strength of any culture throughout all time has ALWAYS been determined by its art and music. Any TRUE scientist knows this.

That being said, your belief is not required to perform this incantation, only your open mind, your time, and your cooperation.

AHURA Z DILIIZA

13 CHAPTER NAME

As you have probably surmised by the earlier portion of this lesson. I value the sanctity of the minds of children and honor the role of Mothers. It is this that inspired me to develop an incantation that would insure that no child would have to endure the experience that I myself had as a child. Forgive my dramatic air in introducing you to this next segment...

You see, as a child with telepathic abilities growing up in America, I did not suffer the feeling of pain, separation and alienation from other children as it is often shown in recent popular television shows. I thought that everyone could see! I learned that they could not. However there was no trauma of feeling of the other children thinking that I was crazy. I did not dye my hair black, wear shadowy make up and black clothes and huddle somewhere in a fetal position wondering why I was so different. I knew that I was different, so if anything I felt special.

My reason for giving the next spell is in fact not because of people, but because of the gifts that I bear. I could hear things that no one else could. Know, feel, and yes, see things that others around me could not. During the day this was great. There was just one downfall; my dreams were horrendous! My sleep was tormented by creatures that no movie could even come close to depicting. These dreams tormented me for years until finally, I discovered a way.

I needed the earth and heaven itself to help me. I remembered that whenever I was trapped in a state of suspension by one of the creatures that inhabited my dreamworld (scientists in their insistent mediocrity and unwillingness to acknowledge the existence of things they cannot explain with a ruler or microscope label the effect of my experience "sleep paralysis". I am the one that experienced this, and will look any scientist in the eye and challenge that weak summation) I could not move or even cry out for help. The creature told me that it was taking me to the devil. I struggled to move or utter something, some sound that one of my siblings would hear and shake me awake. Unfortunately, this darkness that the creature placed me in was like cement. I was fully aware of everything that went on around me, I felt everything and I was NOT ASLEEP!!!

So, I did the only thing that I knew to do. I needed a super hero, and the most powerful one that I knew was Jesus. No, not the floaty, lily pad-walking, cracked out guy that you see in all of the paintings and pictures. I needed Jesus the demon fighter, the liberator, the one that was going to help me!   I summoned all of the will that I could and with all of my might I screamed out in my head, *JESUS!!! HELP ME!!!*

I was again able to move. My mouth was unsealed and the weight on my chest was removed. I sat up in my bed and did everything that I could to keep myself from screaming.

As I grew I would hear accountings of these night terrors from others, and so decided to do something about it.

The spell that I will teach you is designed to stop the terrors. They will stop for you and yours as they did for me.

Now, while I do not expect children to remember this, I DO expect you parents to place the plight of the afflicted above your skepticism just for a time. What is it that we like saying nowadays, *children first?*

After the child takes their evening bath, light one single candle and place your hand on the heart of the person that you are performing the spell for. Close your eyes, and address that which you call your "higher power"and recite this three times:

Heaven and earth to my delight,
Shield and protect me against the night.
Keep the dark creatures away from me,
Cause the night-sickness to flee, flee!
Circle of fire now answer my call,
And burn the dark thoughts that would cause me to fall,
Father of heartbeat, Mother of breath,
Keep all oppression away from my breast,
Feathers of Angels now cover my bed,
And keep the dark nightmare away from my head,
Shine your light now to make me clean,
Blind those demons that would cause bad dreams.
Now do I thank you for setting me free,
And give my allegiance to thee, thee!

Kiss the child on the cheek and assure them that they will sleep peacefully. If needed, be willing to stay with them until they are surely asleep. If there is even the slightest hint of stress in the person sleeping, gently caress the cheek and call their name until they wake up and ask if they are okay. While I am aware that the steps that I am giving you take time and involvement, you the parent must realize that your child (or loved one) is undergoing an extraordinary event, therefore YOU must be the extraordinary parent. I have designed this incantation to be recited by mother or father. If it is for an adult then read it as if you are the parent to that adult, even to yourself. By reciting this spell you get the opportunity to break the night terror and to be to your child that which I did not have in human form – the hero.

14 TOTEMIC

In this next segment I will address a question – well, two questions – that MORE than frequently I have been asked: *"What is my animal totem?"* and *"How do I get in touch with my totem?"*

Now, most of the time when a person asks me what their animal totem is, they already have in their minds what they would like to hear. As a teacher of mysticism it is my job to answer in a way that is informing and thought provoking, and so I look at them as if concentrating on the aura of totemic energy that surrounds them. I reach out to them slowly and answer in a low shamanic voice, "Your totem is... a DORK FISH!"

This goes over well... usually. That is, until someone actually believes you, and says "What's a dork fish?" (this really happened).

In all seriousness what a totem is, is a spirit guide usually – but not always – in the form of an animal. The word "totem" comes from languages spoken by natives of this country that is now called America. The totem is to symbolize all that the individual or family is; the strengths, gifts, characteristics and intelligence of a tribe. For instance, if a person has very catlike qualities such as flexibility, stealth, and sharp yet articulate reflexes, it is an elementary step to assume that person has a feline totem. Now this does NOT mean that your totem is a cat just because you like them. A spiritual guide has very little if anything to do with whether or not you like them.

I have on one occasion met a person who's totem was obviously a wolf. Her movements, gaze and mannerisms screamed wolf, but she insisted that she MUST be a cat because she loved them so much. Her stubborn resolve caused her to deny herself all of the benefits that the wolf totem had to offer her. Those benefits being strength, speed, extraordinary awareness, and resilience. Not to mention the spiritual ability of collective consciousness!

Likewise I have encountered a person that found the very thought of having an eagle totem repulsive. Ironically the person had very poor eyesight and was deathly afraid of heights. Even to stand upon a ladder would cause him to sweat and become nauseous. Had he simply accepted is totem, which was in fact the eagle, he would have benefited from the gifts that the eagle offered such as VISION, fearlessness, freedom, accuracy and the total and complete absence of phobia.

My point here is that when it comes to the totemic, what we like or dislike has absolutely *no* relevance. That being said, if we can see beyond our bias we may unlock the spiritual potential hidden within each of us. Remember that we are indeed related to the animal kingdom, and therefore entitled to the very attributes and gifts that they have to offer. A simple ceremony will help you get in touch with your totem...

Usually there is a drink that must be imbibed before performing the ceremony. In the interest of prudence I will give you a beginning version of this. A stout tea with a few drops of Tabasco will do (remember this is an introduction). Find some material; green for earth, fertility grounding, birth and life and purple for ceremony, wisdom, magic, royalty and initiation. From these materials create robes, simple ones that will cover your body entirely.

Make sure that the moon is in the proper phase (waxing, close to full being the best), and begin.

If you are outside and have privacy build a small fire and scroll a circle around the fire far enough away so that it is safe. If you are inside, a group of candles will do. Take your tea and drink. Begin a rhythmic step going clockwise, as is the course of nature. If it helps you, have someone play a simple beat or bring an apparatus that will play music with a constant uninterrupted beat, so that it enhances your mood and moves you to form a dance (while remembering to keep your rhythmic step around the circle). Music that has no vocal imprint works best as it will not interfere with your chant.

Once you begin to loosen up and "feel the beat" so to speak, begin chanting softly at first and then elevating your voice these words (I *learned this spell in Spanish, and in English. However, what I personally found is that the spell was much more effective when chanted in Spanish. You do what works for you*):

Desde alla   (dez-deh ahya)
hasta aqui   (ahsta ah-ki)
animal aparesca a mi (ah-nimal ah-paresca ah mee)

Translation:

From beyond
quickly come
animal spirit to me.

Repeat this over and over allowing your body to move as it wants to. Let inhibition be the thought and energy that you express. Soon, your magic should make itself apparent. Your movements will begin to emulate the movement of an animal. Soon after that you should receive a vision of your animal. Let it and yourself merge, and commune with it. You will know within your being when this has happened. Bring your dance to a close (or keep going). Thank the Goddess and your totem for blessing you, and douse your fire.

Repeat this when you choose to (as nature LOVES a good party). Remember, if you choose to have others be present while performing make sure that they are of like mind, as only those that are part of your clan should be present and participating (NO LOOKY-LOOS!). To deliberately misquote a phrase, "The clan that changes together, stays together".

I know you will enjoy this as I do. Welcome to the TOTEMIC.

15 GAIA CHANT

Now that we have entered into the segment of Unicorn Light Mysticism that can also be called tribal or clan magic so to speak, let us journey further. The next incantation is known as *Gaia speak* (Gaia being the name of Earth, and all of those that live on and within her.)...

Gaia speak is the language that is spoken if you took every representation of every language that is spoken within her and combined them. Within this language is the power and energy of the divine nature of the planet itself. This "speak" is done usually by a clan, or tribe. Chanting a litany in Gaia speak creates a veritable storm of spiritual power which expresses the first principal for which energy should be used. Remember again that energy is to be used for either *creation* or *procreation*. As we are in fact, in the image of both God and Goddess, we have the ability to do both. Procreation is what we do when we have children. Creation is what we do when we give birth to our dreams or goals. Either way both principals must be present, as is with mother and father. Part of my personal heritage is Maori and this culture reflects the sacredness of the mother spirit of Earth, or Gaia.

It is this culture that will allow me to properly teach you this *speak*. I want to make it clear that the language of the Maori, although part of Gaia speak is not Gaia speak. So, for those of you that speak fluent *Te Reo*, you may recognize a word here and there but it is only one of the languages found within Gaia speak.

In the Maori culture there is a ritual that is performed by the men that is called *Kamate Haka* or *Haka Taparahi*. This chant calls forth the power of the ancestors and fills us with the power to become victorious in battle. Though there is so much more to this ritual (which I promise to address in later classes) let it suffice to say that it is a very powerful event. *Haka* can be used in many events and for many reasons, sometimes for welcoming, celebration, competition and for power. While in many cases *Haka* is done by the men of the tribe, or clan, there are some forms that are performed by the women. Likewise in this Gaia speak it is women that are featured prominently as there is no more powerful force than that of the Goddess.

The women of the Maori culture express the very essence of that power that we seek to bring forth. I have watched as Maori women were transformed with a clap of their hands from a warm and welcoming charm that is found in all women, into a beauty and power that was almost, for lack of a better word, terrifying. Though men participate here they merely lay the ground work on which the women will form the great whirlwind of pure magic. This performance will transform women into the very image of Gaia herself. Having been involved in this ceremony I have witnessed first hand the awesome power of that which I am about to show you. So without further delay....

In order for the chant to work you must completely invest yourself. Dress in whatever you believe to be "tribal dress" (I will leave this up to you as creativity here is imperative). Choose a rhythmic beat, slow but primal. As in *totemic* allow yourself to sink into your own primality. Feel your body. Forget the constrictions of normalcy and be free. If you have at least one male that has rhythm, request of him to participate. If he has honor and is a willing witness to strength and beauty personified he will gladly accept the invitation.

On the next two pages are the words that you will chant. Learn them first and then recite them to a simple beat. I have presented a way for you to pronounce the words here:

- When you see the letter "a" it is ALWAYS pronounced short, as in the word "art".
- When you see the letter "i" it is always pronounced as in the word "in"
- The letter "e" is pronounced as in the word "leg".
- The letter "u" is pronounced as in the word "June".
- The letter "o" is pronounced as in the word "stone".

If you follow these vowel guide lines you should encounter no difficulty. You will not be able to do it it first correctly, but with practice you will master Gaia speak. Until then have fun (if you prefer doing it in English, then please do so. Either way you will get what is needed).

Ayo-wa tho ama yaweh an ho,
Pati addonai ho, issa kah kama riate
Shiminah cu ime ime con roo aparita con roo,
Issa cah kama riate.

(men)
Thre min-a secu-ii, ra- i- na- i- katsa,
shan-i ri ra Om-pa, Ruusha, ruusha
kia kia ra ra sho, Uma tama aha sho,
Ashi-ra inah-sho Eeya."

(women)
Mane- Mane- Yake- Toa
noke akuchiri- ee Pati- pati,
ya po ke, neki ori ya ke ya ke
ama Yaweh i-li-ra-ke-he-la- makui
Ri-a-te Ri-a-te hilira- ke Ri-a-te
Ashe-nise a-o-ri-a Ria te Ria-te HO!

Translation:

To you I bow
Mother Yaweh I bow
Holy Father I bow
to you now, and prepare for you
my life make new,
in me, in me shine through,
Holy spirit come through,
all is good and prepared for you

(men)
Heaven has said to me
I am now catching
Gold and silver right now,
Quickly, quickly turn, the spirit key for me,
Mother Father come for me,
I pray God Goddess come,

(women only)
Power, power into me come,
take your home, reside in me,
heal my heart and strengthen me,
and before you I stand, I stand Mother Yaweh,
give to me and I will stand forth, Powerful.
Powerful, I will stand forth Powerful,
give me strength and beauty, make me Powerful
powerful, NOW!

(repeating this last part until you wish to stop) Revel in the
pure power of the Goddess!

Please do not attempt this ceremony unless you have ample time as one can lose all sense of the linear. Have something on hand to eat, and plenty to drink. There is no other caution to give you. Be free, and may Gaia transform you...

16 LOVE SPELL

Okay, for those of you that have waited patiently and with great hope the answer is... Yes! I am going to give you a LOVE SPELL (whoo-hoo yeah!).

For generations we as spiritual beings have sought to answer one question in our lives (and no, the question has not been *What is the secret of life*, or *What is my Universal purpose* or even *exactly who puts the pimento in green olives?* Nope. The question that I hear most often is: *Do I have a soul mate?* or *When will I meet my soul mate? Have I already met my soul mate? Is the person that I'm with my soul mate?* Etcetera, etcetera, etcetera...

A little history is in order I think...

I have performed readings of every sort from the Tarot to simple look-at-you-and-tell-you-what-I-see for a little over thirty years. To the last question as to whether the person that you are with is your soul mate, my answer can only be; *if you have to ask then the answer is no.* My premise? A *soul mate* suggests that one soul is a match or mate to another, just as one of your hands is a match to the other and would therefore not require an outside source to verify the compatibility of them.

The mystery of soul mates is one which many sages have theorized and philosophized about for all time. The truth is that no one can explain what a soul mate is unless you've already met yours. It's kind of like this wonderful fail-safe mechanism that the Universe has provided so that we don't mess it up for each other. Some things truly should be earned.

Even as a telepath I do not have the right to interfere. I can only "light the way" so to speak, which I will do in this segment. Before I do that however, I WILL help you by revealing to you what is NOT your soul mate giving, you at least a fighting chance in solving this all consuming riddle of life (*ahem*)...

Your soul mate is NOT:

• Someone that you have to *work on the relationship* with. If you are with the right person it should not take "work" as those that have chosen toxic relationships will try to convince you. Your soul mate and you should be harmonious and beyond the constraints of what society believes, or thinks.
• Someone that your parents pick for you. We live in an undercover bias that has taught our children to match themselves to another based on eyes, hair, build, race and skin color Fortunately the Universe is not concerned with non-evolved concepts such as racism and is highly capable of sending you one that is of a different ethnic code. You see, it is your SOUL that the Universe is more concerned with, not your upbringing (besides its kinda weird)...

• Someone that happens to wear the same color that you do on a given day. Just because you have the same color shirt as the person walking down the street does not mean that there is a psychic connection between you. Unless of course you share a psychic connection with everyone that shopped at the same store that you did, and if you do, JACKPOT!!!

• A person that you met on "Soulmate.com". Really? REALLY???

• Someone that you have to lower your standards for. I don't care WHAT your mom told you, just because she wants grandchildren (did I mention weird?).

I could go on, but hopefully you get the idea.

Your soul mate is for you. We who are gifted with the ability to *see* should only show you how to attract that which already belongs to you. It is up to you and *only* you to decide whether or not the one that you have attracted is your soul mate. Remember, your soul mate will ALSO know this and does not have to be convinced. Which reminds me:

Just because you *think* that someone is your soul mate does not mean that they are. If someone is treating you badly, shunning you at every opportunity, that is a sure sign that they are *not* and they wont change just because you get pregnant or go to an expensive phony psychic that says that your soul mate has the letter "A" (no wait I mean "O", or "E") in their name. (Now that I have spoken to you like a chastising older brother, allow me to return to my warm lion-king-like manner)...

A love spell is supposed to create in you the energy that is required to bring the one that is most likely to be your match. However, you the performer of the spell must be ready for such a thing. If you are desperate to have someone in your life this is not for you.

You must be willing even against yourself to discipline your mind so that you are ready to receive. In other words you must look for some*one*, and not some*body*. This takes patience and discernment. If you attempt a love spell without either of these the results could be disastrous, for you will only try to control what should always be free.

Remember, a love spell is never to control the emotions or actions of another. To attempt to do so is a violation of free will and thus a violation of the principal of Unicorn Light Mysticism. Besides, you want your love to be real and free. A spell should only make it so that your mate can see you clearly, and you them.

It has often been said that the only thing as innocent as childhood is love. That being said, you approach the love spell like one who would approach the gates of Heaven itself – like a child.

And so, here it is: the LOVE SPELL (please, be responsible)...

Make sure of the phase of the moon. In this case the moon should be in its waxing phase because of the nature of the spell. Remember, waxing moon means when the moon approaches full (for things to come to you). Waning moon means when the moon moves toward the new moon and appears smaller (for things to go away from you).

Gather some roses of two different colors and spread the petals on your altar. Find one good-sized candle and carve the symbol of love into it twice, once for you and once for your intended love. Get two pieces of ribbon (again one for you and another color for your projected mate) and wrap them both around the candle. If you are female then dress and make your self up as you would when going out on a date for the first time with your love. If male then shower, shave and dress in a way that is appropriate for a first date with your love (Guys! A t-shirt, baseball cap and jeans or khakis is NOT *dressed*. And take a shower for goodness sake).

Stand or sit in front of a cleaned mirror. Look at yourself. Light your candle and recite these words softly and clearly as if speaking to a lover...

Roses red, violets blue,
I just want to be with you.
Like two diamonds in the sky,
Our love will always shine.
Have no fear, I am near,
Feel me whisper in your ear,
You and I are meant to be,
Meant to be, meant to be....

Wait quietly. On the very air the sound of a bell will be heard. What you heard is real. Do not question this. Your love is surely on the way.

Speak of this to NO one, for it is between you and the Universe. Once you have finished douse your candle and every night light it and sit with it for five minutes. Be at peace and prepare your life for the new arrival.

And so with this last spell we are in the closing moments of your formal introduction into The Way of The Unicorn. You have been introduced to the elements, your bodies, minds, senses and the dimensions. Although this is just the beginning; your first step into The Way of The Unicorn. You have embarked upon a path of enlightenment that has always been available yet unexplored; *Magic*. True magic is within each and every one of us. You might even say that it is our birthright.

17 CLOSING WORDS

I would like to thank you for your attention. It has been truly an honor to have you in my class, this introduction into The Way of The Unicorn. I promise that the class that you have attended is only the beginning and crafted especially for you. The experiences that you have read are all true and witnessed by clients and students of my acquaintance all over this great country that we call America and the world.

It is indeed my hope that you will continue your education and journey into the world of Unicorn Light Mysticism. By practically applying mysticism and divine principals to your life, using the simple steps that I have given you, you will be able to help yourself and others.

Until our next class, we will contemplate what we have learned and master what we can. Remember, take what you have gleaned and make it your own, for in magic, mysticism and spiritual development that is the way.

It is The Way of The Unicorn.....

Namaste.

ABOUT THE AUTHOR

Ahura Z. Diliiza is a natural telepath, metaphysician and educator. He has taught the metaphysical arts and divine sciences all over the United States for nearly 3o years. He owns and operates Unicorn Cove School of Metaphysics where he teaches people how to improve their lives and evolve.

For information on private classes with Ahura Z please visit:

www.unicorn-cove.com

Made in the USA
Charleston, SC
23 March 2012